MIND POWER

MASTERY

JONNY MACCE

MIND POWER
MASTERY

What is it that makes some people more successful than others?

More importantly, what is it that makes some people happier than others?

Of course, you can always point to luck and you can always point to outside factors. Sure, there is often an element of knowing the right people. Of being in the right place at the right time. Of being born with a silver spoon in your mouth…

But if you constantly focus on the factors that are outside your control then you will never obtain the fullest of your potential. Not only that, but there are *plenty* of examples of people who have beaten the odds. People who were born into poverty, who perhaps didn't have the opportunities that others did. Of course, there are plenty of examples of people who dropped out of school or college and all these people nevertheless managed to become immensely successful.

Likewise, you can have two people in the precise same situation but they might be completely different in terms of how happy they are and how they perceive their 'lot' in life.

The difference? The successful and happy people have the right *mindset*. They have the ability to look at a situation and see the glass as half full. They can spot their opportunities and they can take those and make the most of them.

JONNY MACCE

Having the right mindset allows you to see the best in a situation and thus be much happier *no matter* what kind of situation you find yourself in. At the same time, having the right mindset allows you to spot opportunities that others might miss and to play the hand you're dealt.

In short, everything starts with the right mindset. The right mindset can help you to accomplish more, to do more and to be more effective.

So now the only remaining question is how you *get* into that correct mindset in the first place.

By JONNY MACCE

Would you be willing to leave a review?

It'd really help a ton. The first popular review of this book is probably going to be THE review that people will see for years to come. If you have time to write one today, that'd be great.

I am looking for reviews on Amazon so that I can get some feedback from readers, people just like you! I would greatly appreciate it if you would check out my book and leave me a review.

If you enjoyed this book or feel that it has helped you in anyway, then could you please take a minute and post an honest review about it on Amazon?

Click here to post a review!

Your review will help get my book out there to more people and they'll be grateful, as will

I

JONNY MACCE

clarifying purposes only and are the owned by the owners themselves, not affiliated with this document.

Chapter 1: It Starts With Your Mind

If you have an 'internal locus of control', then that means that you recognize just how *responsible* you are for the quality of your life and your accomplishments. Many people have a tendency to blame others, to blame circumstances, or to make excuses when things don't go their way. Why aren't you happy? It's because you had a hard childhood! Why aren't you rich? It's because you weren't born with a silver spoon in your mouth, or because you lost your job due to lay-offs.

Making excuses is easy but it doesn't get anywhere. The reality is that people have dug themselves out of holes *much* deeper than the one you're in right now – I don't care who you are – and they have come out richer, happier and stronger.

So, what is the all-important ingredient? It's *you*.

And more specifically, it's your mind. *Your* mind is where everything else comes from. Your beliefs, your focus, your concentration, your mood – all of that. What's more, is that where your mind leads, your body follows.

If you are low on energy, then you might be inclined to think that it's time to make changes to your diet or to your training regime. In all likelihood though, it is your *mind* that needs fixing first.

Everything in life is dependent on numerous other factors. Whether you're talking about relationships, about your career or about your financial situation. How can you find your dream job when you don't have the option to leave your *current* job? When you're so broke?

And how can you stop being broke when you are so badly in debt?

But change has to start somewhere. And it starts with you. It starts with your mind.

A better job, starts with the mind.

A better relationships,starts with the mind. A better LIFE, starts with the mind!. Here's a little saying to keep in mind:

The grass isn't greener on the other side, it's greener where you water it!

Time to Change Your Mind

This is all very good and well, but how exactly do you go about *changing* your mindset? How do you take back control, reclaim your happiness and start living a fulfilling and inspiring life again?

The thing to do is to diagnose the problem. What exactly is *wrong*

with your mind to begin with? And how can you fix those issues?

Well, not to alarm you, but there's probably a

lot wrong with your mind. Don't worry though: it's fairly common and it's very much a sign of the times.

I can guess that you aren't completely happy with where you are right now. Maybe you don't like *who* you are right now. I know this because you're reading this book.

If what you're doing right now is working for you then great! But if it's not, or if it could be working better, then something needs to change.

Here are some starting points that can help you see precisely *what* you might need to change.

#1 Responsibility

The first problem that many of us have is that we don't take responsibility for our actions and we don't *want* to take responsibility for our actions.

Now we all know people who don't like taking responsibility – they will blame others and they will make excuses for what they've done. These are the people with the external locusts of control that we have already discussed.

But while this might seem like an irritating problem for people around them, the reality is that this is a much *deeper* issue that affects them more than it does anyone else.

Because a completely refusal to accept responsibility means that you *also* reject your own autonomy and your control. If you believe that nothing is your fault, then you also really can't take credit for anything that goes well. Moreover, it means that you don't have any power over your life and it means that you can't *choose* to change things.

It's not up to you, it's up to chance!

It gets worse too. If you are too used to avoiding responsibility, then chances are that you will avoid taking responsibility for other things in your life too. That means you'll avoid making commitments to people, which might make you feel 'free' but ultimately means you get left behind as those around you settle down into relationships and find fulfilling careers.

It means you'll put yourself forward for fewer tasks in the work place – at least those tasks that have any major consequences. And if you aren't responsible for large amounts of money, then you can't expect to get *paid* large amounts of money either.

Being afraid of responsibility will even make you less impressive, decisive and confident in a day-to-day scenario. When someone asks you to make a decision, you won't want to because you won't want to be responsible for what happens *if you get it wrong*.

And unfortunately, life has made it all too easy for us to learn this lack of responsibility. We are sheltered by so much technology and for the most part, life has become much easier. Our childhoods have also become extended to a massive degree and *especially* in the current generation of youths. These days many of us will stay at school until we are 18 and will then attend college for 3, 4 of 6 years after that depending on the amount of qualifications we obtain.
  Throw in a gap year and some time 'finding our feet' and many of us don't begin our careers until we're in our mid-to-late-twenties.

JONNY MACCE

This was exacerbated by the economic crash of the last decade. Many people leaving college struggled to find work, which left them without workplace responsibilities and very often still living with their parents. Generations previous were likely married homeowners with children at this point.

And it's hard to ditch this mentality. It's hard to stop being a perpetual child. And while there are positive sides to this (it's good for creativity, for dreaming and for enjoyment in the moment), ultimately life will catch up and we won't be prepared. We are too *soft* mentally to cope with the challenges that will come our way. We've lost the ability to be decisive, strong, action-takers.

What can you do to fix it? We'll explore this in more depth in some of the other reports but the key to acknowledge is that you must learn to *accept* the possibility of a less-than-perfect outcome. Accept that there will be times when things go wrong and it's your fault. And when that does happen, be willing to put your hand up and admit it.

That's what it means to be an adult. And that's what will give you the strength to start taking more chances and making more bold decisions.

#2 We Care Too Much What Others Think

Ultimately, number one comes down to doing away with fear. This is another topic we're going to address more over the coming reports but for now let's hone in on one very specific example of fear, one very specific cause

That is that we care too much what others think.

This is something that occupies a *lot* of our thoughts for many of us and something that can actually be quite tiring. Many of us will simply *not do something* if we think it is going to make us look unusual. If we think it will elicit stares.

Not only that, but caring too much what others think is what makes it so hard for us to take responsibility for things: we don't want to seem to be weak or to lose the trust or respect of other people.

You know what the biggest irony of this is? It is the refusal to take action and take responsibility that actually *makes* people lose respect. This is what makes us appear weaker.

Many of us also struggle to go after the things that we want in life because we are too busy worrying about pleasing others. We're so busy saying yes to invitations that we don't really want to go to and spending money on things that we *think* we should own, that we don't have the resources left to spend on things that really matter to us.

And this of course greatly limits what we are capable of and the quality of our lives.

Now I'm not telling you to forget other people entirely and to become an ass. That's certainly not going to improve your life!

But learn the subtle difference:

- ☐ Care if other people are happy
- ☐ *Don't* care what other people think of *you*

This is the most heroic mindset because it means you'll do kind things for people without even telling anyone and even be willing to make yourself look foolish.

But at the same time, you'll be much happier because you won't be living up to the expectations that you believe other people to have.

You'll be able to take more responsibility for yourself and you'll have one less *huge* thing causing you stress.

So how do you make the switch? It is easier said than done of course but the key to getting started is to stop holding yourself to the standards of others and to *start* holding yourself only to your own standards. Judge yourself on your own terms and by your own code of conduct.

#3 We Are Impulsive and Reactive

Perhaps the biggest symptom of modern life is just how badly impulsive and reactive we have become.

And this really is something that has been exacerbated by modern technologies and convenience.

Did you know that our attention span has

measurably deteriorated over recent decades? The reigning view is that this is caused by time spent on the internet. When we read a blog post we can skip across the headlines and the bullet points and then stop reading. Often we'll get our information from YouTube or Twitter – which is limited to only 140 characters!

When we find the piece of information we want, we can close the tab and search for the next thing. It will be there in seconds!

We've become very good at quickly skimming and assimilating information but we've trained ourselves *out* of sustaining our attention and concentrating.

And this is then made a lot worse by all the other things vying for our attention and all the other immediate gratification we get. We have all the food, all the entertainment, all the gratification we could possibly need right at our fingertips. Much of it is free. And much of it can be served up in seconds depending on your internet speed.

Adverts are designed with bright colors and attractive faces to grab our attention. There is noise *everywhere*.

And thus we have become incredibly reactive. Every one of these distractions that leads to reward will trigger a dopaminergic response. Eating a sweet, loading up PornHub, playing a computer game, watching a YouTube video… This reinforces the same pathways in the brain that are present in addicts. And it completely undermines our ability to control our attention and to decide *what* we want to look at. *How* we want to behave.

So, when we sit down to work towards a massive deadline, it should come as no surprise that the first thing we do is check Facebook. And make tea. And grab a snack.

How do you get out of this rut? There are a few ways and again, we're going to delve deeply into all of this. But one of the simplest fixes is to try meditation. Meditation teaches us to take conscious control of our mind, to be more in the moment and to avoid distractions. This can help us to become incredibly more disciplined and focussed and can certainly do away with a lot of procrastination and impulsivity.

#4 We Are Lazy and Tired

The other big problem that prevents us from achieving what we want and that causes a whole *lot* of unhappiness is laziness.

Most of us know what we should be doing but we lack the effort to do it.

When given a choice, we will take the easier route.

In the short-term this is great. It means you get to spend the evening on the couch with a bag of chips watching your favorite trashy TV. But in the long term it means you lack the stimulus for growth. And guess what? Growth is perhaps *the* most important thing we need to be happy.

Because you are never still and stable. If you are not going forward, you are going backward. If you are not growing, you are *regressing*.

If you don't exercise then your muscles atrophy. But likewise, if you don't use your brain and if you don't challenge your mind, then your brain physically shrinks. Worse, you *unlearn* how to apply effort.

But part of this is not laziness. Part of this is stress and tiredness. Because the problem is that we typically lead such busy, stressful and fast paced lives that we simply have no energy left at the end of the day to do anything about it.

Is it any surprise? Most of us commute into work for 30-90 minutes on a train or bus or sitting in traffic in the car. We then fight our way through a busy street into the office where we sit in a cramped, stuffy room and get shouted at by clients and unhappy customers. We work to urgent deadlines and end up staying late, then we make the precise *same* commute back home.

You can add malnutrition on top of this for many of us. Halogen lights too. Loud noises. Air pollution. All these things upset the body and cause *physiological* stress.
These put us further into the fight or flight state and the body simply can't tell the difference.

This *exhausts* us. And that's what makes us choose the fast food in the cupboard and it's what makes us skip the workout. It's also what causes us to argue with our partners and not have time for our kids.

And it's not even *time* that's the issue here so much as energy.
Your psychological energy is a *finite* resource.

So, the first thing you need to do is to start buying yourself more energy. That might mean looking into easier ways into work, or it might mean swapping to an easier job.

It means finding space in your life so that you can stop *reacting* and being in fight or flight. They you can start to become *proactive* and make your way onto your inspire path.

Moving Forward

This isn't even all of it. I haven't even touched on how many of us are also stuck in our own heads, how we're anxious and worried about things that don't matter, how we're ungrateful, or how we don't actually *know* what we want.

But THESE are the things we need to fix if you are going to start getting the most out of life again. This is where it starts. Are you ready?

Chapter 2: Mindset and Emotions – How to Control Your State of Mind

If you could genuinely master your emotions – take complete control over the way you felt at any given time – then *that* would be the **ultimate** technique.

I'm serious. If you could do this, then you would become unstoppable in a fight. You would become relentless in the gym. And you would be able to apply yourself to a task in a way that would previously have been impossible.

I imagine that you're probably rolling your eyes at this point. You probably think I've been reading too many hippy blogs. Maybe reading a little too much fluffy self-help.

But I'm serious. Most people *seriously* underestimate the power and influence of their emotions.

So, allow me to elucidate you and then demonstrate how you can get your state of mind back under control. At least to *some* degree.

Unlimited Strength, Perfect Focus, Incredible
Creativity and Social Skills

That's quite a bold heading right there and you might already be shaking your head in disbelief. But hear me out.

Emotions and Strength

Want strength? Some of the most feared fighters in history were known as the Beserkers. These Norse warriors were so called because of their 'bersker rage' – a mad fit of anger that they would fly into on the battle field. In this heightened and agitated state, they would become almost invulnerable and would also be able to accomplish feats of incredible strength.

There have been more recent accounts of something similar too. Hysterical strength is a term used to describe more recent scenarios where individuals have seemingly been able to dig into an immense reserve of strength at will. This is where the stories of Mothers lifting cars off of their children trapped beneath come in. Likewise, there is a story of a rock climber who managed to bench press themselves free of a huge boulder likely 200KG or more.

Think it's just a myth? Turns out there is a solid scientific explanation for how this might be possible. Under extreme stress, it seems likely that the body produces excess amounts of testosterone, adrenaline and cortisol. These hormones increase the heartrate, focus, awareness and muscle tone and *that* is where the extra strength comes from.

Actually, it goes a little deeper than that even. You see, all of us have limits to our strength imposed by our minds and our biology. When you go to lift a weight, you do so by recruiting muscle fiber– little bands that make up the muscle and contract in order to give us our strength. The most muscle fiber that the average person can recruit at once under normal circumstances is around 30%. The most that a highly trained athlete can recruit is closer to 50%. So, a *highly trained* athlete is only capable of tapping into roughly *half* of their maximum strength. This is what we mean when we refer to a 'mind muscle connection'.

Ever seen someone get electrocuted in a movie (think *Jurassic Park*)? As you know, the idea is that the individual will get flung across the room into the far wall. What throws them? *Their own muscle*. The electricity causes all the muscle to contract at once, which creates such a jolt that the person goes absolutey flying. Imagine if you could *harness* that power and use it to leap up onto a roof!

The reason we can't access so much of our strength is a) that it would likely cause us injury as we would break a muscle, pull a ligament etc. and b) that it would fatigue us. If we were to use *that much* of our muscle power in a single movement, we'd have no energy left for anything else!

But under the right circumstances, being able to dip into these huge reserves of strength is incredibly useful. And adrenaline and other hormones under the right conditions allow us to tap into that power. Studies show that yelling in the gym can actually increase adrenaline and thereby enhance muscle fiber recruitment, resulting in strength improvements!

Now imagine if you could tap into even just 80% of that power at will? Simply by harnessing your emotions?

Emotions for Calm, Collected Focus

But there's only so far that being able to leap tall buildings and punch through walls will get you. In the real world, physical strength isn't really what matters.

This then is where the 'flow state' comes in. A flow state is often describes as a state of calm, focussed, bliss. It is what happens when the world seems to slow down because you are so intently focussed and engaged on what you are doing.

Have you ever opened a cupboard and seen everything fall out but moved in super-fast motion to catch it? That's a flow state.

More often we hear about it in extreme sports – athletes finding their flow and being able to pull off incredible stunts at incredible speeds.

Outside of physical activities it is seen in music. When the entire band synchronizes during a jam, this is a type of flow state.

When you have a conversation with someone that lasts all night, that's a flow state.

When you're writing a book and you write so long that you don't even notice the time passing *that* is a flow state.

Studies show us that executives in flow manage are hugely more productive than those that aren't. The same goes for startups.

So, what *is* flow? Essentially, it's another emotion. Another mental state that is *triggered* by the release of hormones and neurotransmitters. In this case, it is a subtle variation on the fight or flight response, a subtle variation on stress and panic. Here, you believe something is just as important as preventing yourself from getting injured, it is just as compelling as fighting for your life – but it is also *fun* rather than scary.

You have the *entire* attention of your body and mind which brings about a release of excitatory hormones along with calming ones and those related with bliss – such as anandamide. This actually suppresses activity in the prefrontal cortex, triggering a state known as 'temporary hypofrontality'. This prevents us from worrying, from second guessing or from over-thinking. We just do. It's the opposite to how most of us live our lives today and that's why many of us are filled with anxiety, frozen with fear.

Imagine being able to talk up to a woman/man in a bar and deliver your wittiest conversation ever. Imagine being able to talk in front of an audience with passion and conviction and enrapture them completely in what you're saying. Imagine being able to work on the projects that matter to you for hours on end without *even looking up*.
No fear. No doubt. No bursts of anger or unwanted emotion. And this is when our best work is done. This is when we are
 happiest.

Many people try and live their lives in flow as much as possible. The problem is that most of us are full of anxiety and busy with chores and things we need to do. These limitations leave us stressed, anxious and busy and they take our mind *out* of the moment. Our entire body and mind cannot possibly be in-sync when we are worrying about debt, or what our boss said at the office.

Entering flow means being in the moment which not only makes you happy and confident – it makes you unstoppable.

Creativity

Changing your emotions can even make you more creative. The *opposite* of a flow state is something called the default mode network. This is a network of brain regions that spring into action when you are engaged in boring repetitious work or when you are just relaxing. This is what happens when you allow yourself to become completely at ease and let your mind wander.

Now many people give this mental state a hard time. They say that this is when your 'inner Woody Allen' chirps up. This is the opposite to 'living in the moment'. But in fact, this is also when your creativity kicks in. This is the state that *Einstein* was in when he came up with his special theory of relativity (while working in a patent office!).

This is daydreaming and that is when we come up with plans, ideas and more.

No emotion is a bad thing. The answer is just being able to *tap into* the right emotion at the right time. It's about emotional *control*.

Social Skills

And finally, the obvious power of emotion: social skill.

If you want to seem confident, then you need to stop worrying about what others think. If you want to be a leader, then you need to be able to take command, not second guess yourself and not get upset and visibly riled when things go wrong. If you want to engage others and make friends and partners, you need to be charismatic, engaging and entertaining.

All these things are based once again on having control over your emotions. But the thing is: most of us *don't* have any control. Most of us sulk when we don't have a good day and put ourselves in even *more* of a funk. Most of us are scared when things are wrong. When we're stressed, we argue with our partners and avoid important work in the office. We sabotage ourselves, undermine ourselves and struggle to get things done – all because we can't control our emotions.

Taking Control

So how do you take back control over your emotions? There are multiple ways, but let's address two important points: physiology and mindset.

Physiology refers to the fact that your emotions are really an extension of how you *feel*. Emotions describe things like happiness, sadness, anger, fear. We think that these emotions are born from our minds but a lot of the time, that's not the case at all.

Rather, emotions come from our bodies. Emotions come from *feelings* which include things like hunger, tiredness, hot, cold.

The very function of your emotions is to trigger behaviors that will help you to fix the way you feel. When you haven't eaten enough lately, your blood sugar dips. This in turn triggers a release of cortisol – the stress hormone. This tells you that something needs to change and wakes you up and in the wild, this would have encouraged you to look for food.

When you eat, your blood sugar spikes, you produce leptin and serotonin. This makes you happy and content and encourages you to sleep – eventually serotonin converts to *melatonin* the sleep hormone.

So, in other words, the way you *feel* is often the result your physiology and that changes the way you think. You think you're angry because you had a bad day? Possibly. More likely, you had a bad day because you're angry. And you're angry because:

- ☐ You didn't sleep
- ☐ You're in mild pain
- ☐ You haven't eaten enough
- ☐ You've eaten the wrong things

You get the gist? So, one way to change your emotions and to take back control is to acknowledge this. Firstly, recognize that if you're angry, it's probably due to physiological reasons and *it will pass*. At least it won't seem so bad later.

Secondly, seek to change this. Eat something. Sleep. Take the cue. Learn to follow your own rhythms and work when you're *naturally* most productive. Follow the rhythms of the day and get your circadian cycles in check.

And at the same time, look at ways you can directly control your physiology. The very best way? Breathing!

If you learn to breathe correctly (using belly breathing to fill the lower portion of the lungs, then the upper portion) and if you use slow, controlled breaths, then you will be able to lower your heartrate and calm your entire body. This will change your parasympathetic tone, taking you out of 'fight or flight' and into 'rest and digest'. Try it the next time you feel overly stressed, overly competitive or worked up after an intense workout – your heart rate will slow and your mind will grow calmer.

The other tool you can use is something called CBT. Now we're looking at the psychological, self-talk aspect. CBT stands for 'Cognitive Behavioral Therapy' and this is a popular form of psychotherapeutic intervention used to treat phobias and other anxiety disorders.

The idea is to look at the content of your thoughts. The self-talk that you give yourself to work yourself into a panic, or to calm yourself down. If you are thinking things like "I'm worried I might fall off that ledge" then of course you are going to be scared. If you think things like "I'm grateful for my wife" then you will be less likely to feel unhappy with where you are in life.

It goes deeper than that of course. You can use CBT to challenge long-held beliefs and to break negative self-talk habits by challenging your thoughts and testing your hypotheses. This is called 'cognitive restructuring'.

In the short term, you can use CBT techniques in order to more honestly assess your state of mind and your emotions and to then change the way you feel about a situation.

So if you were stressed that you had a deadline you couldn't meet and it was ruining your evening, then you might use cognitive restructuring in order to assess the thoughts making you stressed and replace them with more productive ones.
For example, you might consider:

☐ What is the point of being stressed? Will it make matters better?

☐ What's the worst case scenario? Would it really be that bad to tell the boss you can't finish work on time? Are they expecting too much of you anyway?

    ☐ When was the last time you did this?

    ☐ Are there other ways you could lessen the blow?

    ☐ What would you rather pay attention to right now?

Combine this with controlled breathing and bring your focus to the thing that is most *useful* to you right now.

In the long term, you can use CBT in order to bridge the gap between your thoughts and your physiology. You see, your physiology and your emotions are designed to drive you toward desirable states: sex, food, shelter, love, success, social acceptance.

The problem is that the tasks you need to accomplish often *don't* get you those things in the short term. In the long term, entering data into that spreadsheet helps you keep your job which helps you pay for food and keep your family!

But in the short term, it just means *more boring paperwork*.

So now you need to remind yourself *why* you do what you do. And you'll do this not only with words but with visualization. *Picture* where you want to be. Picture the wealth you want to have, the success, the satisfaction. Then remind yourself that the things you do today are actually *driving* you toward the things you want.

This is when your heart and mind will finally be on the same page.
  And that's when anything becomes possible.

Chapter 3: Mindset and Focus: How to Control Your Attention

Attention and focus are the two things you need more than anything to accomplish… well *anything*. If you want to get work done, tidy your room, get into shape or make any other kind of meaningful change in your life, then you need to sustain your attention on that task long enough to make a dent.

But this is where your brain may not like to play ball. And we've all been there. We've all been trying to focus on an important job and get work done, only for our mind to keep wondering, or for us to keep finding things to do that are *more* fun.

How many times have you sat down to get some work done, only to get immediately distracted by Facebook, by Twitter, by the news, by a computer game. We've all been there.

And how many times has this distraction ended up costing you money, costing you time, or leading to you to miss out on opportunities?

Or think about this: how many *hours* do you think you've racked up through procrastination? How much more productive do you think you could have been if you *hadn't* spent all that time browsing the web?

This is one example of why focus and concentration are so important. But this is just *one area* that is affected. In reality, your attention or lackthereof is also responsible for a *wealth* of other things. Your ability to focus your attention is partly responsible for your mood for instance. If you can keep your focus on one thing, then that will prevent your mind from wandering to dark places and it will prevent you from getting angry.

Attention is also crucial when we're driving – if your mind constantly wanders off, then you could lose a fraction of a second to brake when the car in front screeches to a halt.

It's crucial in conversation too. If you want to be liked and if you want to influence others, then you *need* to be able to focus on what they're saying.

Focus and discipline are tightly related. It all comes down to your ability to decide *what* your brain is going to do. It means making your mind, your emotions and your body work *for* you. Work *toward* your goals rather than against them.

And in this guide, you're going to learn to get the monkey mind under control.

The Neuroscience of Attention

First, let's focus on that 'sustained attention' that we talked about. Your ability to stay concentrated on a single task without letting your mind drift and without getting tempted by other activities.

When you engage in this kind of behavior, you are actually using a specific part of the brain that is known as the 'salience network'. This is a network of different brain regions that work together in order to decide what is important and then to direct your attention toward that thing. Of course, this is all internal – all represented by activity across neurons. As far as your brain is concerned, that car coming toward you is no different from the things you're dreaming about.

So how does it decide what to pay attention to? It appears that this is regulated by a part of the brain called the anterior cingulate cortex. This can direct our attention using two 'routes' through the brain. These are the 'dorsal attention network' and the 'ventral attention network'.

The first type of attention represents our conscious decision to pay attention to things. When you decide that something is important and you *need* to pay attention, then you will release certain hormones and neurotransmitters (such as dopamine) to denote this importance. Your attention will then be actively driven via the dorsal attention network to that activity.

The ventral stream meanwhile is reserved for situations where our attention is stolen away from us by something interesting or shocking. This is a reflexive form of attention that is largely out of our control. So, for instance, if you hear a loud *bang* noise from behind you, this will likewise trigger the release of neurotransmitters and that will force your attention via that ventral route.

Putting Science Into Action

So that's how your brain works when it comes to attention and I'm sure it's all very interesting…

But what good is this to you? How can you actually *use* that science in order to get the results you want? How can you make sure that you are paying attention to the right things and not easily distracted?

Well, the first thing to recognize is this key difference between ventral and dorsal attention. There is a constant battle going on between the conscious decision to direct your attention and the unconscious urge to look at things that are loud, that are colorful or that are moving. What's more, is that your ventral stream is also going to be activated by physiological things: like hunger, tiredness or discomfort. If you badly need the toilet that will nag away at you and it will steal attention from what you're meant to be doing.

So, if you want to improve your ability to concentrate on the things you *want* to concentrate on, then you need to make sure that you aren't being distracted by *other* things that will steal your attention away. You need to prevent the ventral stream from detracting
from the dorsal stream.

So how do you do that? One option is to try a technique used by the CEO of WordPress, Matt Mullenweg. His trick is to find music that he likes and then play it *on repeat*. The idea is that this can end up becoming so familiar and predictable to the brain, that it effectively tunes it out thereby creating a kind of 'sensory deprivation'. It's like a ticking clock, except that the *only* sound you hear is that clock. Not only that, but using music you will still get the other benefits of a high tempo and of having your mood boosted.

It's similarly important to make sure that your physiology isn't going to end up distracting you. To do that, you need to keep your environment free from distractions and you also need to make sure that you are warm, comfortable and well rested.

You can also make your work *more* interesting and *more* engaging. Remember, your ventral attention likes things that are loud, moving or that seem threatening or like they might offer a reward. Author Tim Ferriss explains how he will often put things on TV and watch films on silent that he already knows well *while* he is working. The benefit of this is that it gives him some color, some movement and some attention to hold his attention. I do something similar: I often watch people playing computer games on silent. Doing this means I have something colorful, interesting and exciting to engage my senses but these things aren't enough to prevent me from being able to think about the work I'm doing. It basically keeps my head in the right direction!

Another tip is to make sure you have plenty of energy. Concentration and focus actually requires a large amount of energy and studies show that as our energy dwindles, we start to lose discipline, focus and control. If you are low on energy, you are much more likely to act impulsively. Much more likely to get distracted by sounds and by things that seem more interesting. And much more likely to simply become too tired to want to focus anymore!

So, you need to keep your energy levels up throughout the day. Part of this comes down to taking well-timed breaks and letting yourself rest. It also comes down to making sure you've eaten lots of complex carbs to provide healthy, slow-release energy. Likewise, you should exercise regularly and you should try to avoid stress as much as possible.

You should never consider *any* aspect of your brain power as being independent from the rest of your mindset or your lifestyle. Everything you do impacts on everything else. If you are stressed tired and harassed at work, then you can't expect to perform your best *out* of work!

Entering a Flow State

There's one more thing you need to do to make sure you pay attention to the right thing though, and that is to give your brain incentive. You need to make sure that your brain thinks that you're right – that the thing you're trying to focus on truly *is* worthy of your attention.

Your brain is built for survival. Over thousands of years, it has helped your ancestors to do this by focusing on the things that are most threatening or that may yield the most reward. You focus on the fire building behind you, on the lion chasing you and on the tree filled with delicious food.

In the modern world, we are driven by immediate gratification (cake in the fridge, Facebook) and by things like sex and social status. We want to rise to the top of our social groups andNimpress our family and friends because this is what we needed to do to survive back in the wild.

Now comes the problem:

In order to be successful and to get that sense of accomplishment, you need to do well at your work. To do well at your work, you need to impress the boss. To impress the boss, you need to enter data into a spreadsheet.

But the problem is that the two things are too far removed. Your ventral network has no interest in something as dull and unrewarding as data entry – despite the fact that it can help you to accomplish things that will ultimately make you better and more accomplished.

The opposite of this can be seen in the near-mythical flow state. A flow state is a state of mind that we can enter where everything else seems to fall away and we become purely focused on what we need to do.

If you've ever played sports and time has seemed to slow to a standstill while you perform with incredible speed and timing – that is a flow state.

If you have ever been so lost in work that you forget to get up to go to the toilet, eat or even look up from your desk – that is a flow state.

Even fantastic conversation can be described as flow.

And all of this comes from one simple fact: in flow, we think that what we're doing deserves *100%* of our attention. Snowboarding, having a fascinating conversation or working on something that truly *inspires* us can all do this.

And this triggers measurable change in the brain. The frontal region of the brain actually shuts down, leaving us to act purely on instinct and reflex, while being intently focused on the world around us. We literally 'lose ourselves in the moment'.

So how do you trigger this state when doing the work you *need* to do? The answer is to focus on that motivating reason behind what you're doing. To focus on the *why*. To remind yourself that your passion has driven you to do this.

So for instance, if you are currently working on data entry then you might picture what life would be like if you *did* become executive. Or if you *did* eventually earn enough money to go travelling. This is a means to an end but it is important too – doing this work well, getting it done quickly, will ultimately allow you to live your dreams.

The other important tip is to always do your

best work. Try to find what's interesting in what you're doing. Forced to write something that you aren't enthusiastic about? You *must* be able to find some aspect of that work that does inspire you.

Or perhaps you can simply introduce some kind of twist that will make it more interesting. Maybe you need to change the way you approach that writing to make it more engaging?

And if you find it more interesting to write, then surely others will find it more interesting to *read* as well.

Working Memory

Finally, the last piece of our puzzle is working memory.

What is working memory? It is a type of memory that is used to store information temporarily while you work out problems. For example, if you were doing long multiplication in your head, then you would use working memory to 'carry over' numbers. Likewise, if you had to write down a phone number, then you would use working memory to store the number in your head until you got a pen and paper.

Working memory has often been thought of as a 'storage' container that is eventually sorted for trash or items that belong in short-term and long-term memory.

More recently though, it has been discovered that working memory is really just a form of attention. When you use 'working memory', what you're really doing is simulating something in your mind – imagining yourself saying a number or seeing a picture – so that the information persists even when it has gone from your senses.

And this is used for far more than just holding numbers in your mind. Working memory is likewise used when in conversation to recall the topic of conversation. It is used during sports to visualize the positions of all the players on the pitch. It is used during writing to hold concepts in your mind as you write.

If you train your focus then your working memory improves. And if you *train* working memory, then your focus improves!

So how do you train working memory?

The simple answer is by using it. Playing chess involves simulating movements several ahead of what's happening on the board and this requires a form of working memory. The game 'Rumikub' does something similar, as does the children's game 'pairs'.

You can also enhance your working memory by reading and actually by playing computer games. Computer games have also been shown to enhance decision making, focus and much more – so they're actually very good for you.

The best tool for enhancing your working memory of all though? And therefore the best tool for enhancing focus? That has been shown by *countless* studies to be meditation. When you meditate, you are simply instructing your brain to focus on one thing or *nothing*. This is an exercise in practiced focus only now you're blocking out or refusing to react to *all* distracting thoughts. If you can become good at this, then you will greatly enhance your ability to decide what you focus on and how you react to any given situation. Studies also show that meditation increases your IQ, it thickens your grey matter and it generally makes you smarter, more alert and more in-control of your own brain.

Finally? Practice focusing on the thing you need to focus on. Sure, it might be hard to concentrate on data entry now but if you are strict and you persist, it will eventually become much easier.

Chapter 4: Mindset and Wealth: How to Grow Your Wealth

Can you really 'think yourself rich'? I'm here to tell you that it is not only possible, but that it is also actually the *best* chance you have of making a lot of money.

Many of us dream of living in a large luxurious house in a sunny country, we imagine wearing smart suits that exude power and confidence and we *wish* that we didn't have to make so many hard choices because our funds can't support the lifestyles we want to lead.

If that sounds familiar, then you need to make a change. And as with ALL things, that change starts with you and your mindset. If you want to be wealthy, then what are you doing about it? And is there any chance that you may, in fact, be going about it the wrong way?

Wealth and Your Career

Ask the average person in the street what they would hypothetically need to do in order to become richer and 99% of them will tell you the same thing: get a better job.

Okay, fair enough. They are not *wrong* per say. Indeed, getting a better job won't *hurt* their income and that in turn will likely mean they get richer… at least a little.

But in fact, this is not the whole story. And what's more, is that this isn't even the *main part* of the story.

Wealth and salary are not inextricably linked. They are related sure, but only to a small degree.

If you wanted to see an equation telling you how to get wealthy, then it would really look like this:

Wealth =

Income –
Outgoings

So, let's say that your income is determined solely by the amount of money you are making at work. Even in that scenario, you still have another, equally as important factor. That is your outgoings.

If you earning a cool million dollars a month but you also waste a million dollars a month of lavish holidays and on nights out and clothes, then you are ultimately not going to be very well off. Rather, you're likely to lose money over time.

But if you are earning a more normal $2500 a month but you only spend $500, then suddenly you are saving $2000 per month.12 months, you'll have $24,000 saved away. That's a decent

 down payment on a house!

So, you now have two options. Two ways to get richer. One is that you seek to get a better job and increase your income and the other is that you save more money and spend less.

How to Spend Less

When I was at university, my summer job was working at a yacht club. Specifically, I was a waiter in one of the restaurants there that was actually paid for and owned by the clientele of the club. The club was located in Sandbanks, England – an area that is also sometimes referred to as 'millionaire's row' because it has among the most expensive real estate in the world along the seafront.

So, these are people who own yachts and who belong to a club that is situated in one of the wealthiest parts of the world. Suffice to say that they were not struggling for cash.

And of course, what many people would point out to me is that this should likely result in pretty big tips!

Except that's not what happened. In fact, I received some of the worst tips I have in any job. I had a lady call me over to secretively give me 20p (around 30cents) for my hard work. She literally told me to buy myself something nice. And this is bearing in mind that it is standard practice in England to tip 10%. The meals usually cost close to $150.

I told my Mum this and her response was: how do you think they *ot* rich, dear? Makes sense. Look, I'm not here to tell you you should become stingy with tips. But what I am telling you is that the wealthiest people recognize that every little bit adds up and makes a very big difference in the long run. Your aim now is *not to fritter*.

That $3 coffee you have every morning on the way to work is actually $15 over the course of a week. $60 over a course of a month and $720 over the course of the year. That is a *tiny* amount and that's before we have even considered all those other things you likely pay for that you don't really need. Maybe your Spotify account, Netflix, 100+ TV Channels, gas for the car for all those trips you don't really need to make. It adds up.

Worse are all those larger purchases we make on an impulse. These are things like clothes that we think will make us look smart, games consoles, PCs, overly advanced phones.

How much did your phone cost you? If you're on a contract, then chances are you'll be paying $700 or more for it. Now ask yourself how much *more* that phone really does than something for $300. Do you really need the fastest processor around? Considering that even an old phone can play everything in the app store?

JONNY MACCE

Do you really need a 30 megapixel camera? Or a 4K screen? Can you even *see* the difference between 4K and 1080p?

The real problem here is marketing, the internet and other people. We have unfortunately been conditioned to associate these items with success and to find them highly desirable. We want to get the latest phone, car, computer etc. because it looks so *sexy* in those adverts. But the reality is that these things don't really bring us happiness.

Likewise, we are told that we need to buy a large house, go on lavish holidays. Is this really for us? Or is it so that we can *look* successful to others?

I'm not telling you to cut back on all the things that make you happy here. There is *no point* in having wealth if you aren't going to enjoy it and have a better quality of life for you and your family. All I'm telling you is to make sure you are certain of what it is that *does* make you happy. And that often means deciding what you don't need and what you should be prioritizing.

Have you *always* dreamed of a beautiful big house? Then why not stop going on those big holidays for a while? Why not stop buying widescreen TVs? And how about considering getting that big beautiful house in a less expensive area?

Heck, if you move to Spain, then there are places where you can live in a five bedroom home with swimming pool and roof pool and it will only cost you $200,000. You could almost buy that in cash and think about how much money you would start making then once there was no mortgage!

Conversely, if all you want is to travel the world, then you can change your accommodation to something less glamorous. How about moving to quiet neighborhood and living in a spare bedroom for a while? Your outgoings will be low, so you can enjoy going on more holidays and still save up that wealth.

Know what you want to achieve with that money. Know what wealth means to you and then you can focus on being more efficient with your money.

Financial Modelling

This will also help you to set up a budget and/or a plan. If you know how much you have coming in and how much you'd like to be making per month, saving per month and spending on things that make *you* feel wealthy per month, then you can create a budget that will help you to reach that point within a specific timeframe.

This then is where you can look at those small things you can cut out to save money.

If you have a spreadsheet that contains *all* your income and all your outgoings per month, then you can look at what kind of impact cutting coffee from your routine would actually make. You'll be left with a total profit at the end of each month and you can decide how much of that you want to put into savings and how much you intend to spend on other things. You can even set up standing orders in your accounts so that money saved automatically gets transferred to a savings account.

With such a spreadsheet, you can then multiply the savings you are making by any given number of months and see projections of what your finances are likely to be at certain points in the future. Need more money for an upcoming expense? Then look at something else you can do to cut your expenditure. This is called 'financial modelling' and it's a powerful tool for building your wealth rather than just letting it 'happen' without your direction or input.

A Couple More Ways to Save Money

And what if you have run out of things you can cut in order to save money? What if you are living on as little as possible?

A few other options include changing your providers for bills, selling off old items, or even moving money between accounts in order to receive bonuses. A friend of mine does this religiously and will even take out credit cards with 0%APR, just so that he can put all of that money into an ISA and then make profit on it. If he gets a cash incentive to signing up for *anything* then he will sign up! And he never buys a new piece of tech or even clothing without taking one of the older items to sell and thereby offset the cost.

Something else to note is that if you have a dream of a wealthy future, then you might need to 'be okay' with living a little more simply for a while in order to get there. You need to put the work in now, to reap the rewards in the future.

And this is hard because it often once again means forgetting the conventional signals of wealth and success. Once again, you have to do this *for you* and not be worried about what others might think.

So for example, if you want to someday have a beautiful home, one of the very best things you can do is to live with your parents if they will let you. Sure, it's not glamorous and it's not fun… but if they charge a small amount of rent you'll be able to save *so much* per month that it will help you to get on the property ladder MUCH faster. You could then buy a smaller home in a less attractive area but flip the property to make a big profit. You need to put in the graft and have an eye on the future.

Likewise, you might need to learn to stop trying to demonstrate your wealth and stability to friends. Have you ever met up with a friend and eaten in a restaurant that you can't really afford because you want to see them and because it is embarrassing to suggest eating somewhere cheaper?

As you can imagine, this isn't exactly conducive to getting wealthy quickly! Again, you need to be *willing* to tell them that you can't afford it and to go elsewhere. How about you suggest they meet you at your house?

Setting Up Revenue Streams

Next come the revenue streams.

We've seen how you can actually become richer without changing your job, simply by spending less.

The other strategy is to become wealthier by having more than one income stream. Once again, your salary isn't determining your wealth!

So, what might this mean? One simple option is to take on

another job, such as a weekend job. If you are happy to work on a

Saturday, then you will have potentially $150 extra to spend each week! That's $600 per month or $7,200 per year! Save that and in a couple of years, you can be living in a nice house – or you can use it right now to *feel* that bit wealthier and wear those fancy clothes.

This is a big sacrifice though granted. So, what would be better for most people would be to earn money online for instance. Tim Ferriss describes creating a 'muse' in his book *The Four Hour Workweek*, which is a small online business that generates a passive income.

This can be as simple as finding an affiliate product (a product that you sell for commission) and making a simple website recommending it, then sending people there with ads. This is *very* low maintenance but can potentially make a fair amount of money. You could try matched betting alternatively (a form of betting that ensures you can't lose – it uses only the free bonus amounts that you get given for signing up) or you could look for a simple online job. How about selling photography online? Working as a writer or a web designer? Or, like a friend of mine, try commentating on sports for websites?

You can also make money from arts and crafts of course and sell some things you make on the side, or you can buy and sell items in bulk on eBay!

Then there are the other options that work *offline*: these include such things as renting out rooms to students, such as mowing the neighbor's lawn, cutting hair, teaching an instrument etc.

All these options will help you to make an income that will be *additional* to your current income. Not only does this of course give you a better total, but it will also help to make you more 'resilient' so that if anything ever happens with your main job, you'll of course still have *some* money coming in.

Another tip? The more you make, the more you'll make. Try to look for investment opportunities, whether that means buying a second house and letting it out to someone else, or whether it means moving to an area that you know is up and coming.

A strange thing to think of here is board games. If you've ever played Monopoly, or any other game where you have to amass a kind of resource, then you might have found that it pays to invest wisely early on. To get the card that will pay out just a little bit every round, or that will prevent you from *losing* a little bit every round. These seem like small changes in the short term but over the course of the game, they ultimately put you in a position of great power and help you to win decisively!

It's the same in real life. Make a few right choices that will build up over time. Know what you want. Be patient. And avoid the

temptation to splurge on the short-term gratification. That is how you get into a wealthy mindset!

Chapter 5: Mindset and Business: How to Achieve Success in Your Ventures

When we think of success, one of the images that comes to mind is often one of a business man (or woman) decked out in a suit, standing at the top of a high-rise building and looking out over the streets below.

We associate business with success in this way for a number of reasons. Firstly, success in business often brings money and riches. Secondly, success in business suggests a certain level of skill and ability and tends to yield a higher status and importance as a result.

For all these reasons, business and success go hand in hand in our minds and for many, those are the *specific* heights that we are aiming for.

But is business success *really* what you want? How can you go about getting it? And what might you unwittingly be doing wrong that could be sabotaging your own success?

In this guide, we'll take an in-depth look at what it means to be a success in business; and how you should go about getting there

Be Careful What You Wish For

The first thing to remember is that you should be careful what you wish for.

For many, the idea of success in business is a very romantic and idealistic one. It's something we might spend a lot of time daydreaming about. But as is very often the case, the reality isn't always what you might have expected.

And it might not even really be *your* dreams that you're having.

Let me explain.

Many of us associate success with business. We've already explained this and it seems to make sense on the face of it.

But *another* of the reasons we hold this association in mind, is that we have been trained to think this way. Over many years, we have seen images of successful people almost *always* wearing suits and wielding power. This is how success is depicted in the movies and in the books. We think of the film *Limitless* or maybe *Wolf or Wall Street* (despite the fact that *both* these movies were really lessons *against* seeking too much power, too quickly).

Maybe you want to make your parents proud? Maybe you plan to follow in their footsteps?

The image of success that your *grandma* has is linked to business as well, after all!

But this can then lead to your downfall. If it means that you then chase after things that don't really bring you joy. If it means that you become the head of a big delivery company, or of a corporate legal team.

Maybe it means you become a procurement manager.

Whatever the case, you can end up taking a stuffy job and being a 'suit' and attempting to get rich that way. You'll start at the bottom, put in the hard graft and the work and climb the corporate ladder.

But is that *really* what you want?

Not only are you now facing years – possibly decades – of working hard with very little reward, but you're also going to be working *toward* something that may not be all that gratifying.
Sure, the pay is good when you're standing in that high-rise… but
do you really want all that responsibility?

And do you feel all that passionately about the product or service your company is providing?

The price of success is often that you end up staying late – until 8pm or 10pm – that you have to deal with people shouting at you down the phone and that you are responsible for millions of dollars.

All so that someone can get their boring parcel delivered on time. Or so that a dubious business can avoid a lawsuit.

Is that really your image of 'success'?

And what do you spend the money on? Expensive clothes? A car? Was it really all worth it?

In many senses, this is *not* really success. And not only that, but if you take this route. If you climb the corporate ladder, put in the work and do your time, then you actually *won't* be as successful as you possibly could be.

Think of any *massively* successful businessman. Richard, Branson, Bill Gates, Steve Jobs, Mark Zuckerberg, Elon Musk…

How many of them started a boring job and then 'worked their way up'?

No: they started passion projects. They looked for things that no one knew they needed yet. They innovated. Trailblazed. They came up with completely fresh and novel ideas.

And because they did that, they were able to have breakthroughs that no one could have imagined: reach heights that were truly unprecedented.

The Strategy

So, here's the strategy. Learn to separate 'income' from 'wealth'. If you read the guide on the money mindset, you'll see that the two absolutely *do not* go hand in hand.

Then learn to separate your status at work from your personal sense of pride and accomplishment. You know what? If you write a brilliant novel in your spare time and *not one person reads it* then that should still be just as rewarding.

So, I want you to take some time out. To find your passion and to follow that path. But do it on the side. And view your day job as what it is: a necessary evil to help you get by in the interim.

Over time, you can turn that passion into a way to make money. Then maybe you go part time. Then maybe you go full time. Then maybe you quit your day job.

Why Passion is *Crucial* for Success

When Elon Musk created SpaceX, he was not the massively well- known name that he is today. Musk was a relatively unknown name whose mission it was to encourage the private sector to venture into space. No small task.

But you know what? Musk did it. And his explanation – one of his explanations – was that he aimed big. Many of us feel that we need to reign in our dreams and goals. We have been led to believe that aiming too high will end in disappointment, will make us look foolish.

But the reality is that aiming high is actually *precisely* what you need to do. Because when you aim high, you inspire others. When you have something exciting to say – and when you are clearly excited about it yourself – then people listen. It's so much more inspiring to hear someone tell you they want to go to space than it is to hear someone say… they're a hairdresser (though if that's

JONNY MACCE

your passion, there's nothing wrong with that!).

If you're reading this, then there's a good chance you're in the internet marketing industry. Let's say you are for now.

You might have a plan to launch a website, sell an ebook, make some money.

There are two ways you go about that.

One is the cynical way. The way where your heart isn't in it. The
way that you see *time and time again*.

This approach involves looking for the hottest new 'niche' in the market. Whether or not that's a niche you're interested in doesn't really matter.

Then you buy some content, maybe hire

someone to write some, maybe pump out a little yourself by just regurgitating what you already can find online.

Then, you lace into that content as much SEO as you possibly can. You do everything you can to make the site sell. You cover it in ads. You call it something like 'The Best Fitness Site Ever'. And you wait for the cash to roll in.

But that *will not work*.

Why? Because there's no passion.

If you have a site about animal welfare and you hire the *very best* writer in the world to write for it. If you tell them to write you *the latest, most exciting, newest* content… then you still won't do well.

Why? Because they aren't you. They can't speak for you. They don't know your point of view. And they probably don't know the topic all that well either.

So, they'll do their research. Learn it thoroughly and try to write something great. But it will be safe. Generic, boring content.

People will visit the site and they'll see that. The site has no personality. No tone of its own. No 'mission statement' or purpose. There is no passion or love behind it and so no community grows behind it. The site dies.

That's why the thousands of low quality sites never make it big.

Think of the sites that *do* make it. Those are sites like MOZ blog, like Tim Ferriss' Four Hour Blog, like Pat Fynn's Smart Passive Income. The Verge. The BBC. Forbes.

These are sites that are written by passionate experts. They are sites that have unique, engaging and brilliant content. And unique, brilliant points of view that are unique to the brand. They have high production values, slick design, thrivingYouTube channels.

Do you see the difference?Think about the sites that *you read* on a daily basis. I bet they are either:

A) Large teams of enthusiastic

professionals OR

B) Single, passionate individuals.None of

them will be spam designed to quickly make

money. None of them will be 'overly seoed"

You can't create amazing quality unless you are *passionate* about the topic. You have to *love* doing it. You need to put everything into it. You have to *want* to spend your *free time* writing articles, answering fan-mail and tweaking the logo. It mustn't feel like a job.

If there isn't a topic for a website you feel that way about, then being an internet marketer isn't for you. You need to find what you *are* passionate about. Your calling.

That is how you become Elon Musk and not 'tired, overworked, stressed Dad who works himself to an early grave'.

Do you see the difference? You can't fake it. You have to love it.

Presenting the Image

But I know what you're thinking: it's all good
and well having the dream and the vision
but you also need the skill and you need
that business persona.

And it's true. If you're going to lead, inspire and
get investments then you *do* need to learn to
present yourself and you do need to learn to be
taken seriously. And this is a skill that will help
you in every other aspect of your life too.

So how do you go about it?

The simple place to start is with the
realization that *you are a brand*. Your name
is your own personal brand and just like any
business brand, it is your job to protect that
brand in a professional manner.

You know how it is *so* important for a
website to be correctly spelled, to have

great design, to pay attention to even the smallest details?

It's the same thing with you. You need to present yourself in a way that inspires confidence and trust. You need to make sure that every interaction that other people have with you is a positive one. You need to present the face of a service that people can trust. You need to gain the confidence that you know what you're talking about.

You do this to begin with by conducting yourself in a professional manner. That means that you put in effort and hard work into everything you do. Whether it's that boring 9-5 that you're just ticking over with, or whether it is a client who is very much 'small time' in your eyes.

If you don't give them 100% of your attention, if you rush things or if you make a silly mistake, then that is a black mark against you. If you say you are going to get a piece of work in by a certain deadline, then you make sure you do that.

You never know where amazing opportunities might come from. And you never know what one interaction might lead to. If you deal with someone in a poor manner, or you do a sub-par job, then word might spread. If you do an excellent job, you just might get offered something.

The same goes for any work that you put out with your name on it. Make sure it is *excellent* quality.

Next, you need to make sure that your presentation is perfect. That means learning to communicate. Learning to present yourself in a professional manner – I highly recommend getting classes to help you with public speaking and elocution. This will help you to get your point across in a way that other people understand. It will teach you to sell yourself, to thrive in interviews and to win clients and backers.

You also need to think about the small details of your appearance. How are your nails? How is your hair? Do you have a nice suit? Are you in good physical shape?

All of this has been shown in countless studies to make a difference. People want to bet on the winning horse and if you look like you can barely keep yourself together, then why would anyone believe that you're going to be able to run a business? Sell a product? Provide a great service?

Again, tiny things make the difference here: things like your shoes, how polished they are, how the laces are tied.

Be constantly improving yourself and investing in *you* in order to make a better impression. Meditate. Get enough sleep. Have enough vitamins and minerals. Be *ready* to take those opportunities when they come.

Springboarding

And learn to see opportunities where you don't expect them. Because it won't always be obvious. Think of Sylvester Stallone who wanted to become a famous actor. He was turned down from all the acting jobs, so he eventually got there by writing a fantastic script for a movie. That movie was *Rocky* and he would only sell the script if he got the leading role.

The rest is history.

Opportunities might present themselves to you that don't seem directly related to your goal. But adapt, learn to see the alternate routes.

Because success in any area can lead to success in another. It builds confidence, it gives you connections and resources. This is called 'springboarding', where you use one 'win' to launch you to the next.

If you turn down an opportunity because it doesn't seem to exactly match your plan, then you can end up missing out on something that could have been huge. Always be looking for that next move. Business is like a massive game of chess.

And once again, this is why you *always* need to put your best foot forward. Making the right impression and protecting the brand *opens* those opportunities. Keep your goal in mind, keep winning and keep taking that next step. Don't let yourself become comfortable. And use the lessons from our *other* guides to get over your fear of risk and failure – to keep taking those chances.

If you do all this, then you never know where

your drive and your effort might take you. THAT is how you become a success in business.

Chapter 6: Mindset and Goals: How to Set, Plan and Achieve Your Goals

Having a goal is a little like having a destination. It gives you something to aim for, it gives you something to target and it generally gives you a structure and a direction that might be lacking otherwise.

So, if you think of a goal as a destination and life as a journey, it becomes apparent that without a goal of some sort, you are likely to be directionless. How can get to where you want to be, if you don't know where that is?

Thus, one of the most important aspects of creating a winning mindset is to identify the goals that you hope to achieve. But in order to do that, you also need to understand *how* to go about writing a useful goal. Because not all goals are made equal and actually, a 'bad goal' can be a very destructive thing.

In this guide, we're going to take an in-depth look at precisely what makes a goal good or bad and precisely what you can do to increase your chances of *reaching* those goals in the minimal time and with the minimal challenge.

Wait… A Goal Can be Bad?

Yes, a goal can be a bad thing. And there are a number of reasons why.

Firstly, a goal can be bad if it is kept vague and if it is used as a tool to help placate yourself. Let's be honest, many of our 'goals' are not really goals at all but rather dreams.

These are 'pie in the sky' ideas that we like but which we make no real moves toward accomplishing.

We are *so often* told that having goals and constantly visualizing them will help us to achieve whatever we want and to be enormously successful. But have you ever actually checked the science? Unfortunately, the research paints quite a different picture. Rather than helping us to get to where we want to be, it appears that goals that take such a vague form actually *hinder* our chances of success.

The problem is that we end up dreaming about what we want and
visualizing it but don't actually go after it!

In fact, it might be that having a goal to visualize is what prevents us from feeling the need to take action. In one surprising study, it was found that *talking* about a goal could actually make you less

likely to accomplish it. Want to lose weight? Keep it to yourself. Want to stop smoking? Don't tell anyone.

The reason for this is simple: once you've told someone, you already feel 'ownership' of that goal. You already feel as though it is a part of who you are.

This is a problem because if you now think of yourself as someone who is fit or someone who doesn't smoke, then you're likely to feel as though you don't have to make any major change to your lifestyle. You're *already* that thing, so why bother?

It may well be that visualizing a goal or a dream does the very same thing. When we picture ourselves rich, when we tell ourselves the narrative that one day this is going to be the case, suddenly we remove the incentive to take action. As far as our *brains* are concerned… we're already there!

While it's not a nice comparison to draw, this always makes me think of Auschwitz. There, the Nazis had a large sign that read 'arbeit macht frei'. This translates to 'work makes free'. In other words, the objective was to provide the prisoners in the camp with just enough *hope* to keep them working it was enough to prevent them from trying to *take* that freedom.

In your life, work doesn't make free. Just like it didn't back then.
If you want to be free, you need to change your approach and you need to *take action*.

How to Take Action

Okay then, so how exactly does one go about taking action? The answer is to come up with a plan. This is very different from a goal because it tells you exactly what you need to do.

Yes, that means that you *do* need a goal. You simply have to learn the *difference* between a goal and a plan. You have to recognize that a goal *on its own* isn't enough.

And in fact, 'goal' is really something of a misnomer here. What you need more than a goal is a vision. A vision is something that inspires you, it is something that gives you the motivation and the drive. A vision is what makes you wake up in the morning.

But it is also abstract. It is hard to quantify. And it is hard to know precisely how you should go about *getting* to the point you want to get to.

That's where the plan comes in. The plan is what bridges the gap between where you are right now and where you want to be. And the very best plans are small, they are measurable and they are directly within your control. The best plans are usually made up of lots of much smaller goals, each of which will represent a

stepping stone toward where you eventually want to be.

Don't worry if all this talk of goals, plans and visions is a little complicated right now. Over the rest of this guide, we're going to demystify what all this means and we're going to figure out precisely what you need to do to get to where you need to be.

Creating Your Vision

So, the first thing you need is the vision. This is what many of us once referred to as a goal. It is the 'dream' if you will.

You might already have one. In that case great, you can skip straight to the next section!

But there's also a chance that you don't *know* precisely what you think your vision should be. This is something that often gets overlooked in self-help texts and other advice. So often we are told to 'go after our dreams' but what if we don't know what that dream is?

Many of us would say that we don't want to tie our dream to our job. We don't want to work toward a career because we aren't *career focused*. Other people might feel that they don't want to limit themselves to just one dream. What if you want to be a rock star *and* an actor? A programmer *or* an author?

If you can't decide quite what you want to do and if you don't

know what speaks to you on that important level, then you'll struggle to come up with a plan to get there. We're back to that directionless journey.

Okay, so what you need to do in this case is to simply close your eyes for a moment and imagine yourself in your perfect life. It's five, ten or twenty years from now and everything has gone just the way you always wanted it too.

So where are you? What is the picture in your mind? Are you with your family in the living room, laughing with not a care in the world? Are you standing on top of a mountain somewhere, having just travelled from somewhere exotic? Or maybe you're in a high- rise office, looking out over the city below wearing an incredibly well-tailored suit.

This isn't a specific goal in the conventional sense, but it suggests the 'emotional' content that is driving you forward. Maybe it's success in the conventional sense of the word. Maybe it's money. Maybe it's family and free time. Perhaps it's travel.

Whatever the case, you can now look at how to accomplish those things and therefore work a bit closer to your perfect future.

If you're still struggling, then there are a few more different psychological exercises you can use to get there. For instance, ask yourself what the *best day* you had recently was. When were you last overjoyed? Maybe it was when you bought a new computer, maybe it was when you had a whole day to just relax. Maybe it was when you were on holiday. Or maybe it was just a nice day out with friends.

Think about the things you always wanted to be and the things you always dreamed of when you were younger. And likewise, think about your role models and heroes. What do they have in common with one another? What could you potentially learn from them?

Answer all these questions and hopefully a picture wills tart to form. And a picture is all you need.

Just make sure to assess that picture thoroughly. Too often, we can end up chasing after fool's gold: thinking that one thing will bring us happiness when in reality, it actually just makes us *less* happy. For instance, you might think that the key to happiness is to get a job as a high-flying executive, only to discover that the life is too high-paced and too stressful.

This is why one *last* thing worth doing is to speak to some people who are already where you'd like to be. What is life like for them? How do they feel about it?

Oh and one last thing: you might of course have more than one goal. Maybe you want to lose weight, quit smoking and also become America's next top model. In this case all the goals are related. Or maybe you want to find love and also become the top CEO of your organization. Either way, you can of course have more than one goal and this is probably normal. But what you should do in this case is to place your *main* focus on at least one of those goals at a time. Sure, you can have multiple goals but try to make one of them the 'primary' goal at any given time.

Creating the Plan

So now you have the goal, you need the plan.

To do this, look at where you are now and then look at all the things you would *need* to build the life you are picturing. For instance, you might find that you need a certain amount of money to make your dream of travelling happen. In that case, you need to look at the options available to you to make that money.

Or maybe you want to achieve a certain thing in your career and you realize that in order to get there, there is a certain amount of experience you need to acquire first. How can you acquire said experience?

There are many similar examples of how you might go after a particular goal but the thing to remember in every case is that you need to focus on *small* steps that are just ahead of you. That might mean the next small promotion. It might mean a small upgrade to your home. It might mean developing *any* form of small income.

It might mean writing just the first *chapter* of that best-selling novel.

With that in mind, you're then going to break these smaller goals down even further. Now the objective is to look at the smallest possible steps that you need to take on a daily or weekly basis to get there.

So if your goal is to have a body like Brad Pitt, then that smallest daily step is simple: diet and exercise.

Look around, find a training plan and a diet that works for you, and then commit to sticking to that every single day without one flaw.

Likewise, if your goal is to be a top novelist, then your daily goal is going to be to write X number of words per day. Make the goals easy to accomplish but ensure that they take positive – if small – steps in the right direction.

This is the key target. This is the primary directive. You're going to imagine that vision and let it motivate you when the times get rough. But you are going to forget anything other than the daily target. Right now, that is all that matters

To help you visualize this, here is what it basically boils down to:

Dream/Vision (Overarching Goal) > Plan (Stepping Stone

Goals) > Daily Target (Daily/Weekly Goal)

Changing Your Thinking

So why is this change in thinking so important?

The answer is that focusing too much on a distant goal will make you too *detached* from what it is you're trying to accomplish.

For instance, if your only 'goal' is to become a novelist, then you lack any real structure or any plan. This is going to make it very hard for you to stick too. It's all too easy for you to get lazy, to take shortcuts or even forget all about it.

Even if your goal is more specific and time-sensitive – such as losing 15kg in 6 months – you are still too detached from it. Why?

Because a) you might still think it's okay to

skip a workout or to cheat on your diet one day and then 'put off' the goal. By the time you have 1 month left and you're still no lighter, you might give up. Or what if you stick to the plan as much as possible but you *still* don't see the results you want? How disheartening is that?

So instead, the goal is the target. You focus *just* on the one day. You either succeed or fail. It is entirely down to you. It's entirely your responsibility and no excuses cut it.

But if you keep focusing on the daily targets, you will find that the overarching vision takes care of itself. It's like building a house brick by brick, or taking a journey step-by-step.

Some Final Tips

Just to help you stick to your path, consider a few pointers.

One: keep your daily targets easy to accomplish. Introduce them slowly. Don't be in a rush to get anywhere. It is better that you just start to enjoy exercise than letting yourself get burned out or put off.

Two: keep track of the days you succeed and lose. Jerry Seinfeld uses this technique and calls it 'the chain'. Every day he does what he sets out to do, he puts a big cross on his calendar. This is rewarding and addictive in and of itself and his desire to 'not break the chain' is reportedly enough to keep him from giving up.

Three: use the most practical and proven methods to get where you want to be. You must *believe* in your plan. Why are we willing to go into work every day but not work on a plan we enjoy and that could make us richer? Simple: because when we go to work we *definitely* get paid. You need a similar plan. Something that will help you to *definitely* get where you need to be – at least in your mind.

And finally: don't get disheartened if you miss one day. The aim is not to of course. But if you slip up, go easy on yourself and just jump straight back on that horse!

Chapter 7: Mindset and Body

How many times have you started a new fitness program only to be disappointed? How many times have you promised yourself you would eat less and be more disciplined in the kitchen only to completely abandon those plans?

Are you someone who has been a little out of shape for the last ten years despite your best efforts? And who just really wishes they could get the body they've already wanted? The one they see on the covers of magazines?

There are a few things you may have blamed for your failure in the past: perhaps you thought it came down to the advice. Maybe you were following the wrong training program? Maybe your PT doesn't know what they're talking about… Or perhaps you have unfortunate genetics?

JONNY MACCE

Well, if you have read any of the other guides, then you will know that this is mistake number one: blaming outside factors is a surefire way to ensure that nothing ever changes. In order to make a difference in your life, you need to start taking responsibility. That means developing an internal locus of control.

And it *is* your fault. Here's the harsh truth: even the *worst* training program in the world is going to make a difference if you stick with

it. If you have the most unfortunate genetics and the only thing you change is to go for one run a week, or to eat one less snack a day; then you are still going to see *some* difference. Sure, it is much better to have a good training program and to do your research. But in lieu of that… *anything* will work. So, stop blaming other factors!

The problem lies with you. But more specifically than that, the problem lies with your mindset. You possibly already guessed that from the title of this guide.

So now let's dive into the issue and see how you can change your thinking and change your results for the better.

Where the Mind Goes, the Body Follows

So, the biggest problem a lot of people have is this lack of responsibility. That, and a lack of conviction. Many people who claim to want to lose weight or build a toned, muscular body, will sonly *really* be interested if they can do so without actually putting in a huge amount of work. The irony is that they don't even realise that this is how they feel!

The first sign that this is the case, is if you find yourself procrastinating. How do you procrastinate when it comes to working out and getting into shape? Simple: you read. You spend ages reading about all the best workout programs, you read about all the different diets, you develop a fantastic plan, you join a gym and then you wait until the perfect opportunity – when work is quiet and when you don't have any other commitments – and *that* is when you deign to begin your training.

But here's the thing: there is never a perfect opportunity. Life doesn't *do* perfect. Life much prefers to be awkward and difficult and if you try to wait until everything is calm and nothing is in the way… well then you're going to be waiting a very long time indeed!

The whole reason that we do this, is so that we can *feel* like we're making progress. Simply by determining that we are going to workout, we feel as though we've done something worthwhile.

And in fact, this even removes some of the pressure so that we no longer feel we have to make the effort!

JONNY MACCE

There are actually studies that demonstrate this. These studies specifically looked at whether or not we should tell people our goals when we set out do something worthwhile. Often, the advice you receive is that you *should* tell people goals: that doing so will make them concrete and real and will force you to stick with them.

How has that been working out for you so far?

The reality – according to the research – is that telling people your goals actually *releases* some psychic tension. Telling people your goals makes you feel that 'fitness' is already a part of your personality. And as such, you actually don't have to put in the real work! Ironically, telling people goals makes you *less* likely to accomplish them.

If you want to tell someone your goals so that you will have a little bit of morale support and encouragement, then tell *just one* person your goal. But otherwise, keep it to yourself. Think about that day when you take off your shirt at the beach and everyone sees your incredible six pack for the *first time*. Let that motivate you!

And to prevent the possibility of you looking for outside excuses as to why you aren't in shape, it pays to hunt down the most effective and simple strategies to get into shape. That's what we're going to look at in the next section.

KISS – Keep It Simple Stupid

How do you lose weight through your diet? The problem is that the answer varies just *so* much depending on who you ask. Some people will tell you that the best way to lose weight is to start eating less. Count your calories and then make sure that you consume fewer calories than you burn. This way, you can maintain a deficit and be forced to burn fat stores. Makes sense.

But another blog will tell you something different. It might point out that counting calories is actually difficult to the point of being nearly impossible. And not only that, but it's also boring and sure to put you off after a while. Worse, it says nothing of nutrition or appetite. If you just eat fewer calories, then technically you can lose weight by eating only donuts. Which would also destroy your health and leave you hungry and malnourished…

So, what do you do instead? According to this crowd, it's more useful to focus on keeping your carbohydrate intake down. This will help you to prevent blood sugar spikes and will avoid 'empty calories' (if you avoid the processed, simple carbs). That way, you are getting only filling, nutritious and whole foods. Great!

Then there are the intermittent fasters and the *low fat* crowd. No wonder you never managed to lose weight!

The other issue is that almost all of these diets are complex, they are hard to follow and they are unsociable. They often involve spending large amounts of time in the kitchen cooking and they can get expensive.

What is the most important part of any diet? Simple: that you stick with it. There is actually *no point* in starting a diet unless you can sustain it indefinitely. If you start a diet and give up in two months, then you will put the weight back on!

Okay, so let's simplify.

None of these diets is wrong. They all have good points. The problem is they go too extreme in one direction. As is so often the case, the 'middle way' is best.

In this case, the middle way means:

- [ ] Trying to eat fewer processed, simple carbs. Avoid the *obviously* bad foods such as crisps, chocolate bars, ice cream and swap them for healthier things.

- [ ] Eat *less*. Don't be obsessive about counting calories and trying to work out what you need to eat every day, but just eat a little less than you normally would.
- [ ] Don't be afraid to go a little hungry. Sometimes the easiest way to eat significantly less is to drastically reduce one or two meals.

☐   Find ways to fit your new diet into your routine.

One strategy that I highly recommend for losing weight, is to eat less at breakfast and less at lunch. These two meals make it much easier to cut down because they don't tend to be social. While your dinner might be something you have with family in front of the TV, with your partner, or out with friends; lunch and breakfast tend to be eaten quickly around work and commuting. Thus, you can eat more boring meals and you'll be less likely to get tempted by the more indulgent options.

Okay, so what about your training? This is a little more complex, seeing as the best kind of training will depend very much on your current physique and the type of body that you are interested in developing. You will likely train differently depending on whether you want to build muscle or tone down for instance.

That said, weightlifting is something that can benefit a huge number of people – including women who want to get lean and toned. Muscle is metabolically active, meaning that when you become more toned, you actually burn more fat even when you are resting!

The other useful thing to recognize is that when you tone your muscle, you can hide fat by pulling it in and you can even make your skin appear more taut. Got stretch marks? Dieting isn't actually what you need and neither is cardio – it's muscle tone that will hide this!

Doing a little cardio is important too though, for weight loss and for your general health. Now, you might be tempted by HIIT workouts. These are 'High Intensity Interval Training' regimes that involve sprinting for short amounts of time and then alternating that with brief periods of rest.

The allure here is that it is reportedly very time saving and very efficient. You can use this training to burn fat and increase your health in a fraction of the time.

But at the same time, what many people miss is that this type of training is *far* harder than it is often made out to be. This takes a huge amount of will power, dedication and a basic level of fitness to begin with. It is *not* the best option for most people starting out. Not only that, but running or swimming etc. can actually yield benefits that other types of exercise simply can't.

So instead, I recommend starting jogging short distances, swimming or running. You can do this once or twice a week and combine it with a generally increased amount of physical exercise during your day. Walking more is one of *the* easiest ways to start improving your health and fitness and burning more calories in a day.

The workout I specifically recommend is this:

- ☐ PPL – Push, Pull, Legs (train pushing movements one day, pulling movements the next and legs the next all in the gym)
- ☐ 30 Minutes of Cardio
- ☐ 3 x Long Walks

Add this into your routine in the way that suits you. That's three gym sessions, one cardio session and a few long walks which can be tied in with your commute, trips to the shops to get milk etc.

The most important aspect of your mindset here though? Making sure that you don't overdo it.

Whether dieting or working out, one of the biggest mistakes we tend to make is to try and get the change *immediately*. This impatience is another aspect of our mindset that can prevent us from reaching our goals. People want to see their abs tomorrow, or this summer. They want to have massive biceps in a few weeks. Thus, they take up intense training programs because they want to feel like they are 'doing something'.

So many people will begin running and try and go 10 miles or more in their first session. Or they'll 'only' do five miles but they'll run *fast* the whole time. It's painful, tiring and exhausting. They come to the conclusion therefore that they 'don't like running'.

The reality is not that they have a problem with running but rather that they have started with too much too soon. The same thing happens in the gym.

JONNY MACCE

So *instead* what you should aim to do is to begin your training in a light and gentle way.

Start out by just running 1 mile at a slow pace. In the gym, maybe just try a few different exercises on low weights. Do this for a while.

The aim is not to lose weight or build muscle in the first week. Not even in the first month. Your *first* aim should be to learn to enjoy the activity. Do it for you. Do it for fun.

Over time, you'll build up your health and fitness naturally as you do. It's impossible *not* to do that. And as you do, you'll find yourself running further and faster and lifting heavier as a result. But don't rush it. Just enjoy it. Your MAIN goal is to make this a part of your life.

Goal Setting and Energy

And with that in mind, consider carefully the way that you are going to set goals.

What too many people will do with their goal setting is to focus purely on a distant end result. Maybe they want abs by the time summer comes around. Maybe their goal is to lose 2lbs and fit into their dress.

This is the wrong way to think about it though, because it gives you much too much flexibility and means you can make excuses. You might decide to take it easy tonight and to try harder to tomorrow. It's also too much out of your control, leaving plenty of excuses for you to make.

So instead, I want you to make your *goal* simply to train every week. This is a goal that is immediate, in your control and immediately rewarding. Every week, if you manage to train at least once (or twice, you set the parameters) then you have succeeded. The abs, the dress, the biceps… these are not goals.

This is the *vision* and this is what will motivate you to *accomplish* your goals.

Finally, I want you to keep energy in mind. Energy is finite and you only have so much of it. If work is leaving you exhausted and if your commute is stressful, then you aren't going to have much energy at the end of the day to work out. So, conserve that energy and carefully consider the ways you can maintain it or increase it. This is why nutrition is very important. It's also why you need to make sure you are getting adequate sleep, giving yourself opportunities to rest and generally making sure your life *outside* the gym is healthy and nourishing.

If you are coming home every single day with absolutely no energy and you feel achy and stressed, then no manner of training program is going to help you. Meditate, take holidays, use supplements and sleep more. And if none of that works then consider leaving your job for something less stressful.

Ultimately, one of the biggest and most important aspects of having the right mindset is knowing how to prioritise. Your health and happiness *should* take priority. If you are never going to be in shape because of your work, learn to accept that and then *leave* your job. It might be the only way to get what you really want from life.

Chapter 8: Mindset and Your Life: How to Live an Amazing Life

Have you ever felt as though you should be getting more
Do you ever feel tired, stressed out, or overworked?

Has your health and vitality suffered? Do you seem to be completely unable to get afloat? Perhaps you feel like you're just treading water…

All this can eventually start to get you down. This is not what we were promised. Perhaps you always pictured that your life would be different. Many of us assumed we would someday make a lot of money. Many of us assume that we should have much more energy than we do.

And we see people around us who seem to have the things that we want to achieve. We all know people who are polished, who are confident, who look attractive…

Do you ever feel tired, stressed out, or overworked?

Has your health and vitality suffered? Do you seem to be completely unable to get afloat? Perhaps you feel like you're just treading water…All this can eventually start to get you down. This is not what we were promised. Perhaps you always pictured that your life would be different. Many of us assumed we would someday make a lot of money. Many of us assume that we should have much more energy than we do.

And we see people around us who seem to have the things that we want to achieve. We all know people who are polished, who are confident, who look attractive…

We all know people who seem to have it *all*.So why can't we have that? Why is life being so unfair to us?

Well, if you have read any of the other guides so far then you know that this is where you are going wrong to start with. It's blaming your circumstances and it's blaming other people. You have everything you need to live a *truly* incredible life right now. All that is missing is the right mindset to go about achieving it.

You know what's even more likely? You're *already* living a truly amazing life. You already have everything that anyone could ever ask for… but you just don't appreciate it.

As we've learned over this series, your happiness and your accomplishments stem from you. And more than that, they stem from your mindset and the way that you view yourself and your life. They stem from having the drive to go out and get the things you feel you deserve. And from knowing *how* you are going to go about doing that.

In this final guide, you're going to learn how to make some simple changes. You're going to learn how to start fortifying yourself against challenge. You're going to learn to start appreciating all the things you already have. And you're going to learn to master your life so that you can decide *precisely* what kind of person you want to be. *Precisely* what you are going to achieve.

What Are Your Priorities?

The first thing you need to do is to start reassessing some of your priorities. Many of us complain that we aren't healthier, happier or richer but we never do anything about it. That's because – despite what we're saying – we *aren't* giving those aspects of our lives priority.

Let's break down your current routine shall we and see if we can assess the problem?

You're telling people you want to have six pack abs. you're telling people you want to be a successful author or a successful business owner. You tell people that your *family* means everything to you.

Okay then. So, if that's true, those are the things you should be spending the majority of your time on… right?

Instead, what you will probably find is that your lifestyle looks something more like this:

Sleep: 6-7 Hours

Work:8-9 Hours

Commuting:1-2 Hours

Lunch Break: 30 Minutes

Everything else: ~5 Hours

And in those roughly five hours, you need to fit in waking up, getting ready for the day, washing dishes, doing the laundry, cooking…

Now ask me again why you don't have the lifestyle you want?

You claim that your goals and dreams are your top priority and yet you don't live a life that reflects that in the slightest.

This reminds me very much of the problem with modern politics. So often, we are told by our political leaders just how much money they have managed to save. They'll tell us how they have increased the value of the dollar. They'll boast that they're paying off the deficit.

But is this how we should really be judging their success?

How about much more important metrics like quality of life? Or happiness?

You're doing the same thing in your own life. You're pouring 90% of your effort into your work and coming away completely exhausted. Of *course* everything else suffers

How it Got This Way

Have you ever asked how things got this way?

The answer, while it might not be very pleasant, ultimately comes down to *fear* and indoctrination.

It's fear because we are driven so often by a

fear of our partners leaving us. By a fear of debt. By a fear of not being able to put a deposit on a house. Of being single in our 40s and missing the boat to have children.

This means that you are motivated by the stick rather than the carrot. You are focussed on running away from all the things you don't want, rather than *toward* all the things you *do* want. And this really isn't helped by the media and by the way we're brought up.

This is where the whole 'indoctrination' part comes in. I'm not a conspiracy theorist. I'm not here to tell you that this is a deliberate move on the part of the government or any such thing.

BUT it is nevertheless the way most of us are brought up. We are raised to believe that we are born into some kind of debt. That we owe this debt to society. That hard graft and work is something to be proud.

Meanwhile, we are taught to want all kinds of things that are just out of our grasp. These include widescreen TVs, lavish properties, expensive looking cars and more. We work toward these things, we work because we're afraid of debt, and we work because it is what society expects of us.

But let me ask you this: is there really any inherent value in work *itself*? Working toward a good cause is *of course* a good thing. Working to support your family is likewise to be applauded.

But those people who proudly state that they've 'never missed a day of work!' or who retire in their 80s, or who talk in a generally proud fashion about the work they did stacking palettes.

It's nice they're proud. Really it is. But here's the sad part: if they didn't come in, the world would keep on ticking on without them. And even if it didn't, the worst case scenario is that someone would get a palette late.

Meanwhile, wouldn't it have been *much better* if they had looked after their health? If they had spent more time with their family?

If they had pursued a passion and written a beautiful piece of music?

Work in itself should be a means to an end and certainly *not* a means in itself. Work only has value as long as the end product has value. And even then, it's not worth sacrificing every other aspect of your life for.

Lifestyle Design

The simple cognitive shift I want you to make here then is that you are not living to work but working to live. It's a cliché I know, but if you actually follow that advice through to its logical conclusion, then you find yourself with something akin to lifestyle design.

Lifestyle design is a way of life that simply flips traditional notions of work on their head and instead focusses on building a lifestyle you can be happy with. You decide what it is you want to accomplish, who you want to be… and then you change your career and other factors in order to fit around that lifestyle.

For many people, this will mean becoming a digital nomad. Thanks to modern technology, there is no need for us to work from a stuffy office or make a long journey into work. Instead, we can simply load up the computer and work from home. This affords an amazing amount of freedom, allowing you to work from wherever you like and *whenever* you like. Many people will take advantage of this by travelling the world with just a laptop and working from coffee shops. That's lifestyle design and that's being a 'digital nomad'.

But it can also mean something much smaller. It means looking at the promotion that comes with so much extra responsibility and it means asking yourself if it's worth it. Wouldn't it be much better to spend more time with your family and *keep* the job you've got?

Alternatively, maybe you take on that job but you negotiate having one day off so that you get a whole day to yourself. Or perhaps you take on a part-time job and a side-income instead. Maybe you conclude that in order to follow your passions, the best option is to become a garbage collector so that you can be free by 2pm in the afternoon. Need more money? Then get a smaller house!

It can even mean that you choose to move home somewhere that you'll be nearer to work so that you have a shorter commute. A shorter commute means 30 minutes extra to yourself per day. Maybe you decide to pay for a cleaner so that you can have a beautiful home!

There are so many variables here that you can play around with that you don't *need* to take the most obvious route through your life. You don't have to follow the predetermined path that has been set out for you by society and you don't need to keep making life *harder and harder*. Some More Changes Choosing to design your own lifestyle and take back control is one way to start getting what you want from life. But there are a few others too that will help you with this.

One cognitive shift is to know your worth, to stand your ground and lose the fear.

Another cognitive shift is to recognize that time and money are both interchangeable. This latter point means that if you are getting paid more but you are also *working longer hours* then you aren't really getting a pay rise at all. The only way this would count as a pay rise is if you got paid more for working the *same* hours.

So, if you're being offered profession up the ladder but it involves staying later at work, there is an obvious answer: you'll just take the pay rise thanks!

This is where knowing your worth comes in. You see, many of us are afraid to ask for more money, or are afraid to increase our rates. We think if we do that, we'll lose work and we'll end up homeless. Again: lose the fear. This doesn't happen. If you are providing a good service to someone, or if you're a good employee, then you can afford to charge more.

Think about how much they're earning thanks to you and how much they'd lose if you *stopped* working for them.

You have the right to charge more. And not only that, but it is *common* for wages to go up regardless of responsibilities. So, if you feel you need more money then don't be afraid to ask for it. And if they refuse? Then you look elsewhere for a new employer or new clients.

As Tim Ferriss says: ask for forgiveness, not permission. Ultimately, you are worth what you think you are worth. If you put a price on your head that is too low, then you can work incredibly hard for no reward. Keep looking. And keep learning.

And here's one more thing: don't wait. Don't wait for life to get better. Don't wait until you're old and retired. Because life always throws you curveballs and the stars never align. The only way you can live a better life is to start *right NOW*. And don't tell me you're too old: you're never too old to be the person you always wanted to be.

So if you've been putting off going travelling because of fear, because of opportunity and because you worry that life won't be there for you when you get back it is time to buck up your ideas. Take charge and go *now*. This is the only way you'll ever go. Work will be there when you get back. And if it isn't? At least you've done something truly memorable and worthwhile. What could be more valuable?

It Starts With Everything

Hopefully, some of these tips will help you to start getting more from your life simply by changing your priorities and going after the things you want.

So where do you start?

The answer is *with everything*.

What I mean by this, is that if you want to be healthier and happier and to live a generally better life, then you need to change everything all at once.

We've discussed that your ability to change your life starts in the mind. But have you considered what affects your *mind*?

The mind has a limited amount of energy. Throughout these guides, I've asked a lot from you: to take more responsibility, to lose your fear, to practice discipline, to stay motivated. All those things take energy.

And if you've only got 5 hours outside of work to be productive in, then you're going to struggle. You'll struggle *even more* if you're highly stressed and if you're burned out.

So as you start to put the emphasis a bit more back onto you. As you start to focus on your goals and on the things that make you happy, you can also look at how you can ensure you are charged and able to get the very most out of life.

It starts with simple things: things like getting enough sleep, things like going out in the sun occasionally and maybe things like taking vitamin supplements.

Later it goes on to more profound matters: learning to meditate. Finding a passion. Surrounding yourself with the right people.

Every aspect of your health and your lifestyle will feed back into the way you feel and what you can accomplish. You need to start small and build up the energy you want. Right now you might feel trapped by your circumstances, so find just that small crack of light. That might mean getting a little more energy by taking a supplement in the morning. But if that gives you enough fuel to consider implementing systems to keep your home tidier and that gives you the mental space to start challenging your work-life balance… then it will all be worth it.

And Finally

And finally? Learn to appreciate what you have *right now*.

Because this is the ultiate key to happiness. Te truth is that if you keep dreaming of that widescren TV then you won't be able to escape the hedonistic treadmill. You'll stay in the fight or flight mode, you'll keep pushing and fighting.

And looking forward to a holiday isn't much better. Looking forward to quitting your job isn't that much better either. Do it now.

And meanwhile, learn to focus on what's already just right in your life. If you stop and smell the roses, if you practice a 'gratitude mindset' you'll realize you've probably already accomp

JONNY MACCE

THANK YOU FOR READING MY BOOK!

Did You Like This Book?

Before you leave, I wanted to say thank you again for buying my book. I know you could have picked from a number of different books on this topic, but you chose this one so I can't thank you enough for doing that and reading until the end. I'd like to ask you a small favor. If you enjoyed this book or feel that it has helped you in anyway, then could you please take a minute and post an honest review about it on Amazon?

Click here to post a review!

Your review will help get my book out there to more people and they'll be grateful, as will I.

JONNY MACCE

Thank You

Printed in Great Britain
by Amazon